City of Honesty

Calliope Chapbook Series

Freesia McKee

WATER'S EDGE PRESS
TUCSON, AZ

This collection of poems is a human-made
work of imagination. No part of this book may be reproduced,
distributed, or transmitted in any form or by any means
without written permission of the publisher, except in the case
of brief quotations used in a review of the book.

City of Honesty
© Freesia McKee, 2025
All rights reserved.

ISBN: 978-1-952526-27-5

Published in the United States
as a part of
Calliope Chapbook Series
a collaborative project with
Lakeland University's Literary Publishing class
Editors: Madeleine Wattenberg, Assistant Professor,
Miranda Boswell, Nailah Jones, and Koda Siebert

Water's Edge Press LLC
Tucson, Arizona

Cover image licensed through iStock.com
Cover and book design by Water's Edge Press LLC

NO AI TRAINING: Without in any way limiting the
author's and publisher's exclusive rights under copyright, any
use of this publication to "train" generative artificial intelligence
(AI) technologies to generate text is expressly prohibited.
The author reserves all rights to license uses of this work for
generative AI training and development of machine
learning language models.

Love in a Time of Fascism

I loved you before we had the right to marry
and I loved you after

we learned a continued knowing,
that liberation of our truth is revolutionary.

I loved you in your most brutal history
when you drove me past the softball field

where girls bullied you for being a dyke.
For being a dyke, I loved you

and the women we recognized out
your station wagon's window

on my street on our third date.
I loved you under the thumb of fascism

when it couldn't see us, erased our love,
and when it stared, and I loved you

in all houses, the cockroach apartment
in Florida, in Missouri and Mississippi,

the rural waterfronts of Michigan
and driving through Kentucky,

sleeping together in Louisiana
behind a double-checked, double-locked door.

I loved you through every one of our early protests,
marching in the streets, and I loved you as a secret

from your mother for five years
because, I knew, it was mostly about love

on our rainy nighttime walks with the dog,
when it was dark enough, you let me hold your hand.

I loved you through bad presidents and wannabe dictators,
and I loved you while our friends were shot,

rubber bullets in the street. Back then,
I thought love was protest,

that I could love you through
a demonstration. Even as I knew

myself alone, I thought I could will us
unbreakable, make us suitable for this fight.

Walking for so long into the fires,
I loved you without fully knowing

of the loving lack. Against you
and even against you,

I loved you.
I kept in mind what we were up against.

Body Politic of the City

The metaphor of the politic as the body
               is clearly   of the land

    each blood vessel a wanderer
    in a downtown crowd

    the wild its own kind of city
    the capillary paths
    the forest flaming everglade lungs

The older I get the more I long for a map
of my own body

The more I dream of a compass
that would tell me

the direction of the day
the roundness of time

Once I could hear the city
inside of you say
    it's your turn, your part

I remembered
    you could

    tell me
    what to
    do

* * *

Aging querent :: Advisor
of breath :: Librarian
of plots :: Professional questioner

> will there ever be a city we know
> by heart completely?
>
> when has the brain's collection
> ignited?
>
> unmeasured rise and fall
> of a city's
>   chest of blocks

Unlocked trunk   nearly lost

* * *

After we caught fire
we smelled of it forever

Flame's boundary the edge of the river
Map obscured by turbidity   Fire as feeling

Bowl of water
gone with the water
Scene of sky
obscured by natural smoke

A dozen parishioners
and a fire marshal
        poised at the edge
        of the suburban prairie
        ready with the antidote

* * *

Once the library
inside of you caught fire
There was the feral
There was the mote

There was the scrap
the burnt flake of the last page
of the magazine hot in the compost

The tea mug's moist map
The loose city's art tattooed on intricate streets
The sonnet was no longer

fourteen lines: thatched office building
stitched blacktop lots
your cells never in gridlock

I watched your breath and I watched the smoke

Queer Kid as Glacial Erratic

It was impossible to catch me.
    Then, I was evidence   of a movement.
        Proof of collective direction.

Lodged, a boulder
                in a "field"

not that I'd ever name it—

    (plot)   (lot)   (parcel)

              land—
                  I could've been

bedrock instead. Now,
        I'm formerly portable,

insistent resident,   silt of myself

    lodged like a taproot, a dropstone.

        To those watching,
        I flickered outside of time
rallying myself
 in an open-air spot
 after I was kicked out.

The compression
   of slow movement
      is how I moved.

How when your raft melts

 you see millions   of you   dotting continents.

Yeah. Being me   is like that

            because I'm visible,

not alone.

This Land Will Always Be Here for You

Even if the city falls.

Even if just
in memory.

Even if submerged by polar melt,
even if the city becomes filled,

filled with an old kind of hate. This land's
a prime number, an example of sticking around.

When you are here, you leave
your soft impressions everywhere,

in the oldest parts of the house, in the way
sidewalks wear your shoes,
the way you've been in town

long enough to know
laws are based on limited logic.

Last night, a movie of rain,
last night, igniting your batteries,
and you ran toward the old city's
tribute, longing for recognition

of what this land might mean collectively
though the officials
with their umbrellas and clipboards
had already decided what to inscribe on the plaque.

Official has never meant *accurate*, here.
This land doesn't need a second memory:
    the land is its memory.

Love in a Time of Fascism

We do not want to die in a flood or on a raft or by an agent
       of the state who shoots us on a bridge

       We do not want to be killed at school
       or in a convenience store
or while waiting in line to vote

We do not want the police
       to pull the trigger in their entitled vigilantism
    of this wretched regime

Do not consume us slowly or kill off without thought
       in any nearby decade of silence or unrest

We do not want to die at the decision-making hands
of a man who does not know us
       a man who thinks he does

Astonishing
       all the ways we do not want to go

that come to mind as chaos grips our tongues
       Where anything could happen

We do not want to die before our parents
       not in a protest or war or senseless act

We do not want to run through rubber bullets or teargas
       or languish handcuffed in a van

We do not want our former alderman to kill himself
the night before election day
        If luminaries must die, may it be of old age

We do not want to have to search our books for protest poems
        We hate walking around our neighborhood these days

We do not want to be hit by a driver on our bikes
        or while demonstrating in a public place

and we do not want to starve to death in an earthquake
        hurricane, sinkhole, drought, or rapid-fire overheating

We do not want to reduce to memory or die and be forgotten
        and we do not want to die while waiting

We do not want to die in this world
        because that would end our ability to change it

Yes, we don't want to live in a place like this
        because we do not want to die

Habitat

Too cerebral writing about cities

>City under a cloudless baby
>City inhaling a smoke sculpture
>>Cities gone of fire
>>Cities queered until they're not

This city—like all cities—is
>palimpsest and beach
>computer screen of a million moving images
>rerouted river smoothing submerged histories

Burned out absent city
City of cigarette butts hot
>glue-gunned to a cardboard core
>contoured stacks of discarded filters

City as archeologist
Pillars of right-angled
wooden blocks City as sea glass

Cemetery full of trash
strewn over the deceased
and beloved bereaved

>When they visited
>to do research
>we told them to leave

How macabre or honoring to walk home and think
>about who died here and when

Teddy bear cellophane-taped to a light pole
    City built over burial grounds
    City increasing burial grounds

We city in same
    and unsame ways

How to Face an Active Shooter

describe the shooter
behind
hands visible and empty

safety measures
and
weapons

direct pressure

quiet warning
and
Quick thinking

Commit to your actions
regardless of whether others agree

among the victims
wrought

you may be
safe
injured
volatile

if you
disarm the shooter
use
makeshift

weapons like
chairs
fire extinguishers
scissors
books

Guided Tour

At the threshold, push aside the thick hanging shroud and enter a bright-ceilinged sanctuary, red light shining through the thick panes of the windows, the whole place smelling of the sea. In the corner, she waits for you at a small table covered with purple cloth. Move close and kneel in front of the table. Look at the cup of water, the silver bell, the letter opener made of bone, a single flower reclining in a vase. The table holds small bottles of strong-smelling liquids. The teller shuffles a deck of cards. There's a gold grate on the wall above you. When the teller asks for your full name, give it with a flourish. As the teller continues to shuffle, the sanctuary ceiling cracks, and puffs of smoke billow above. Through the smokescreen, the teller asks what brought you here, what loss. The teller asks what guide you've been following. *If you stay, you'll be the same forever. Do you think change happens in this place?* Small fish start falling from the cracks in the ceiling, sliding through the smoke, wriggling on the wet floor, swimming away as floodwaters rise. *You can stay, or you can go.* Ask why you have only two options, and think, *this is no place for me*. Present your forehead to the teller. Present the teller with the contents of your pockets. Ask the teller to make change. From the corners of the sanctuary, a fierce wind begins to push you toward the door. Spin around and see the teller's deck of cards caught up in the wind, whipping against the walls like leaves in the rain. Do you know how or why your eyes are still open? Where does the teller go? The rising waters push open the door, carrying you out on the spines of schools of fish, birthing you back into the life you thought you'd ridden out.

First Encounter with *Stone Butch Blues,* 2006

As another

      set of hands

           at the factory

I have been an outlaw

           hidden like the gravel in my palms

Un / fenced
      as a quarry

                  Sturdy as the great lake's floor

      I showed up

           Every day

              I went to work

familiar exile

      accumulating   first snow melting on stone

Love in a Time of Fascism

Still Here, Still Queer
markered on a poster board
lying in your hatchback's back seat, accidentally

visible in the parking lot of the homophobic church
that took school-choice tax dollars
so they could make queer kids feel like you had.

It can be an act of love to play a song
or an act of defiance. In your case,
an act of hiding for a paycheck. I went to church
with you the Sunday after protests

and shook the hands of fascists
as you pulled out all the stops.
We kept paying for our beers and granola that way.
We'd come home from church and back to bed,
our queer protest a holy act.

Back then, we were the beginning of fight,
and some of it was the size of our city,
the endless hope there was enough of us
to take on anything.

You and I no longer speak, comrade,
but I wish for your keen and queer analysis.
We ended our dealings before fascism ended,
before the dog died, after I moved
north before it snowed.

And I grieve you, for so long my strongest
allied rally, the one I couldn't stay with
because you couldn't love in ways you hadn't been loved.
Or you could, but only in community,
in the way we were doing or thought we were doing.

Or, was it yet you hadn't been given
enough. It would take years to know.
For years, I wondered how.

Transplants

I wasted away hours
leaning against the base of a distant tree
My hands glowed with hurt
under the neighbor's bright lights vying

I wasted away the evening
my brain's audition a troubled factory
I wondered how anyone could
feel loved completely

I bleached the floor
Every job was odd
I did it again the next day
Hundreds formed a procession near the beach

We waved at the wavers on the bus
My teacher said *you've got to figure out
your critical question* The odds of succeeding
felt devoted and damned

I wasted away the leg for the pedal
my front and back twin relics of wear
My swollen mattress lost her appointment book
I made a new mattress out of old mattresses

I got my life
I whiled it away
in the fish tank the office the gallery the galley
A lock on my bedroom until

I pulled the smooth bough with both hands
We licked ourselves clean like dogs
The wanted signs posted by officials didn't work
a one-way window New wheels new tires

along the highway past the jalopy's rife sirens
The organ pipes screamed a chorus parting
You the mechanic Me with the bicycles
Our peregrination Our other city

I don't want to go outside so instead

I clean my loneliness asking Where's your extra
room and can I sleep in it Can I tell
the truth that now for months I've
wondered if you would say what's really
going on all these pink lights
resplendent above the city as I nurse my drink
and won't you be my lady or put
your notice in lettering
the shelves the menu This place's flag pulls off
inside the bus I'm waiting
in the nearly empty bar and here's
a new address back in the darker room
There are two spots I could write a new
letter and one of them's across from you

The Interstitium's Song

*It looks fluid — something that ebbs and flows, like the ocean.
It is similarly underexplored.*

When I touched you, I knew that you were more than muscle, tendon, tissue, tendon, bone, tendon, foot, elbow, neck, canal, hair, pond, great lakes, soft waist.

Compartments of your lungs released into my ear like a delta.

A switchgrass seed thumbed into the black of a flood plain.

Far above, I could see the shining highways of your body, rings of agate on the ground.

Water connected way to way.

And I could see the bright highways of your body: the bright highway's thorn in mud. The bright highway's face of rust. The bright highway's papilla, subterranean clot.

Button-string space between skin, muscle, tissue, tendon, tendon, tendon, sea.

Tributary clay. Globe encircling globe.

an organ in its own right

What we cannot breathe without:

> Bluebell
> cloche. Petaled
> scab. Lurex
> mycelium. Epithelium
> epithalamium. Quilted
> bloodline. Under-earth
> electric. Deductive
> and amenable.

The body's highways are an interstice.

> *not all researchers agree*
> *with that characterization*

Names for open space:

meadow, glen, field, lot, prairie, plot, valley, parcel, tract
horizon, aperture, ocean, paddock, cave, well, canyon,
coulee, gulch

lea, ravine, trench, zone, pit, pitch, grassland, bay
empty, waiting, placeholder, airy, vast, overwhelming,
endless

opportunity, cavity, unrestricted

a fluid-filled, 3-D latticework of collagen and elastin
connective tissue
that can be found
all over the body

In each space, different features:

    Space between legs: in the room, neither furniture nor person.

    Space between fingers: a chair with nobody sitting.

    Space between songs: every open moment of the road.

    Space between neck and chest: the way a bird finds a space on a wire or branch.

    Space between teeth: every tick of the ocean without a fish.

    Bent space between knee and thigh: a swift flying for ten continuous months.

    Space between us: chorus of first names.

    Space between bridge of nose and eye: impossible sweep of tall grass.

    Space between toes: dented subway cars.

    Space around us: organized antonyms.

a series of spaces,
a highway of moving fluid,
and a previously unknown feature of human anatomy

I could sense the bright highways of your body the day we visited the winter stairs of rock which showed the way ice lays so unmarred on the Lannon stone and stippled on the gravel on the hill I thought *this woman brought me here* all day like when I see your breath rush out and fill the plane a meadow lush with frost which looks like all the blades at once recall your car parked in a valley afternoon of factories and trains near where I'd take my bike up to the trail called Three Bridges by anyone who takes the time to count

    Bridges, which build fragments into roads.

    Bridges, hats of silt, umbrellas of rock.

    Three bridges, you and I and the space that connects us.

Baltimore Bridge

I wish I had taken more risks. The air and white sheets on a queen-sized bed, the harbor of an unknown destination. How she, the city, reminded me of home, standing in the radical basement bookstore, holding *Butch is a Noun* in my hand.

I knew it was funny to drink a latte frothed by an anarchist. I knew the current song was queer and aspirational. The carapace of the bus teemed with interesting people. A woman stretched her arm over a hollow seatback. I sat on the long bus just to look.

Waiting hours on a black leather couch, watching a casual catwalk, observing. My ID sliding out of my pocket, a slick fish over a wet bar. Playing passenger in the burlap seat of a new friend's old car.

> *What I still love is becoming alone*
> *in a city, jagged formstone*
> *revealing what lies underneath.*

One Sunday morning, a stranger carrying her shoes across the street flashed a bright smile. In the open-windowed church, I heard music from the revival down the block. Loud fans rivered over our folding chairs. I played pool night after night. What was this thick beat supposed to teach?

How a city helped me find the spaces I like. How we began. My missing was gone when I remembered to return and retrieve it. How I lost my identity. How I learned a new place. I came back to the basement; I bought a different book.

Someone left *The Poetics of Space* in a brown paper bag on the sidewalk while I was on the hunt for giveaways. I found an anonymous neighbor's journal on a park bench. I returned the next day in the rain and I took it. I sat in my room like it was the bus, believing in the story of another person with such hunger. We began: I learned to read and write. There was no way to get lost. I sewed to accompany a city's unpredictable band. The warehouse of free books wouldn't burn for years.

What Makes a City

This terminal
both departure and arrival:
interstice and actual

no different than a country
Train stations bent
like knees or elbows

Every private lot once public

                     a city not necessarily
                     the presence or absence of people

(a packed remote highway is not
a city?) Not necessarily the presence

                     or absence of buildings:
a dam-flooded valley (no longer a city?)

                     or constellation of tents
(yes, a tent city)

Is a ghost town a city?
                     What's the difference between

a city and a town? In a city

she says you don't have to leave
for any basic need

Queer the train Intervene

Peaked present station
                    (someone else's memory)

We've heard the stories
so many times
it's like
they happened
to us

                    Is every encampment eventually
                    ruined or abandoned? Is a place still
                    a city as long as the recorder runs?

Love in a Time of Fascism

Once we knew which fascist would rule
our lives again, I started missing you long
as when we'd walk our dog into the Florida night,
scheming the protest art we'd make
to prove our love stayed worthy of a fight.

I miss the scrappy kindness in how you woke me
up, hours drawing variations
in strategy. Our love was new,
and I was hungry for you, then,
when we gathered friends in the worker-owned
pub that would close during a pandemic.

That night after an election,
Toby and I cried about men
we would've loved who didn't survive Reagan.
Every kind of death seemed immediate and possible.
In the bar, our friends were making protest signs

on cardboard boxes and posterboard.
Unfurled on a low stage,
you painted slogans on a white sheet
pulled from your bed in a house
you bought when you were closeted.

I've never thought of it, but this gathering
was the only kind of wedding we ever had,
those stacked acts of our resistance repeating
the way straight people celebrated anniversaries—
with the assuring longevity of sanctioned repetition.

This time, I gather my new friends
in a city you've never lived
and see the way, though we ended,
our shared protests never did.

Sonnet for Road A

after Bernadette Mayer

In my pot roast dreams I am always with Aquarius
Spent last night asking my friend to leave
the patriarchal caravan The neighbors next door
can't tell one dyke from another My desire to leave
Milwaukee said We're moving slowly
They didn't see our welcome sign afraid of bees
Today she dug woodchips and left the punk
car Horribly I never knew why it took so long to leave
Left fighting honestly I yoked up heavy with
a certain kind of loneliness They're filming
a movie here I guess we're acting She said
Take all the books you want and let me leave
When I'm not with you just you your hands your hair
To think on all the timing makes me laugh The same
vast neighbors walk the other street You drove me swift
We south Our north we carry

Holy City of Walls

the casements squeezed closed
leaded lights in our own world
we knew we drew near a city
because we saw walls

you picked up a window
placed it into the wall
we were young and we flexibly
entered

the melting spring
   sill and still
   stilt and silt

a city
a table of objects of art

in what kind of city
does one cross the threshold
without knowing the out way
without even caring

half the women
we met carried churches
as closets/with light
through the dalle de verre shining in

go back further
we said before walls

in a forest
beech potash
came glasswork
the walls we inherited

we knew the walls
of the city
ringing walls of windows thank god
thank god well

thank god for her handmade door

Break

this geography
this electricity
this neighborhood of origin

I've walked
  for my few decades

The lake
    exuberant sheets
      of ice crashed and refrozen
    like split wood thrown

I knew how cold this clay gets
  or soft sand in a freshwater pool
My clean vessel
    propped between slick

stones I know what wonder
      does to my throat
  vicarious elevation

All the trails connect,
you basically can't get lost

I thought I knew where I might
      find you
imagined your car in the trailhead's parking lot

I thought I knew how to catch up
      but you were gone

Detours of War

for Robert Burns

We inhabit a world of buildings deemed official
by officials. Downtown,
rivers swim with colorful trash
around the cool blue Federal Building

staid like a bold, unmeltable cube. In 2004, we stood
nearby on Saturday afternoons, bearing signs
against the wars. Years later, we would spot our protests

in a YouTube video. Our signs reflected black and white
and matched what the sky looks like sometimes, or the lake
reflecting its surroundings. We still see the same people

at rallies. One of our friends shares a name
with a famous poet. He's entered the city's secret system
of underground tunnels. *What have you found
down there?* we asked him. He said *Guns.*

We told him we used to sit near the statue
named of him but not for him with other poets'
books. How we were a shivering island

in a lake of cars, willing ourselves
to have come from somewhere
else, longing for a city of honesty.

Someday will be the first day, we say,
when all of this is gone—the statue,
the video, the river, the poets, the book, the guns.
We say someday there will not be war.

Love for You in a Time of Fascism

You have no idea how much
I love you, how much I need your voice
with frost on the grass
and scary morning radio.

You have no idea. With the blusters
that almost swept me off my bike going to work
with the youngest activists we know—no idea
how much I need to hear your heartbeat

through your dance moves.
In your sigh, your coughs, your shudderings,
I hear your breath, and need this solidarity
of presence for as long as you will give it.

The slap of the back door, your bike lock
as you chain to mine, the scraping
of your chair legs, the sound
of steam off various pots of soup

above the punk fundraiser in a basement
where you drop change into the bucket
against another war. You have no idea
when you say you can't focus

on anything else. There are genocides,
dictators and deportations, shootings
in all bleak seasons, your unsure jaw
shaking, so tender and your own.

Is there any way to tell you
how precious, how I hold you a raw jewel,
a pumpkin seed? How much I need
your unsure gait, stilted and aflame.

Your worries, a wall of grapes. I want
to spit the sour out, ferment
every acrid thing
into a cup of liquid drinkable.

I want you to remember there are moments
I need nothing more than your voice
when it is feeble; to know you are a survivor
makes my survival possible.

Special Thank You

I thank the ancestors who worked for a world in which I can write and publish poems like this. Thank you to Dawn, Madeleine, Koda, Miranda, and Nailah for this opportunity to publish with Water's Edge Press. Thanks to the English Department at UWSP, my graduate school mentors at FIU, the chicken tenders dinner group, the poets of Quatrain and the Meltdown, Caitlin Scarano, and my family of origin for more support than I will ever deserve. Thank you, Eva, for inspiring me to write the book that comes next. This is for the ones who fight for our shared future.

Notes & Acknowledgements

"How to Face an Active Shooter" is an erasure of an email from the City of North Miami to residents.

The italicized lines in "The Interstitium's Song" are quoted from a March 31, 2018 article in *The New York Times*.

Craig Santos Perez writes love poems that are acts of global care. His approach inspired the "Love in a Time of Fascism" poems.

Some of the poems in this manuscript have been published individually in literary journals:

About Place Journal: "This Land Will Always Be Here for You" and "Habitat"

Rogue Agent: "Sonnet for Road A"

Small Orange: "Detours of War"

Tinderbox Poetry Journal: "The Interstitium's Song"

Virga: "Holy City of Walls"

Zone 3: "Body Politic of the City" (as "Body Politic")

About the Author

Freesia McKee (she/her) is a poet and hybridist who writes about gender, genre, history, and place. She is the author of two previous chapbooks, *How Distant the City* (Headmistress Press, 2018) and *Hummingbird Vows* (Bottlecap Press, 2023). Freesia works as an Assistant Professor of English at University of Wisconsin-Stevens Point. She has an MFA from Florida International University and a BA from Warren Wilson College.

Learn more at freesiamckee.com.

www.ingramcontent.com/pod-product-compliance
Lightning Source LLC
Chambersburg PA
CBHW020444090526
44586CB00045B/839